Flawed By Design

Also by Martin Zender

*How to Quit Church
Without Quitting God*

*Martin Zender's Guide to
Intelligent Prayer*

Martin Zender Goes To Hell

Flawed by Design

Think your sins are ruining God's plans
for your life? Think again.

Martin Zender

STARKE & HARTMANN

Flawed By Design

© 2004 by Martin Zender

Published by Starke & Hartmann
P.O. Box 6473
Canton, OH 44706
www.starkehartmann.com
*1-866-866-*BOOK

Printed in the United States of America

ISBN 0-9709849-3-6

To my fellow sinners

"Now we have this treasure in earthen vessels, that the transcendence of the power may be of God and not of us."

—*the apostle Paul*
2 Corinthians 4:7

Scene I

A woman crashes into the home of Simon the Pharisee. The town sinner, she neither knocks nor removes her sandals. Whoredom is fresh on her clothes, yet something belying this rests angelically upon her face. Only one person here can appreciate the transformation. The woman hurries to the feet of the Master.

An unusual thing had occurred in the early morning hours of that day, after the last man (the last client) had slipped into the Jerusalem night. As she looked about her cubicle, a dread of the future gripped her. Why should she feel this now? Why tonight? No immediate answer came, yet a vision of her final hours flickered in the flame of her one remaining candle. She would die in this room; which night, she did not know. It would be soon, though. Death would come slowly in a pool of blood, released onto the floor by her own hand. Her sister Mariba would find her. Mariba would scream, there would be a funeral—thirty days of mourning—then it would all be over.

The walls closed in. Stars twinkled outside these walls, somewhere. A sun shone on the other side of Earth, though not for her. For her there was only the shadow cast by her burning piece of wax, a leather ghost running from her feet to a corner, up a wall, across the ceiling, then back to her naked feet. Nothing could escape the cubicle. Floor, wall, ceiling, then back to engulf her. Her hands went to her face now; she was crying.

She had to get out.

Not one other soul occupied the side street where she burst from her home. Urgency along this void of humanity became her silent scream. She would not break down in the city.

Outside the Essene gate, down the valley of Hinnom, up over the aqueduct, then west toward the Bethlehem Road; this brought her to the field. Recently gleaned, dead and quiet, the soil sent coolness into her legs. From above, the heavens lay frozen and mute. Between these two voids she fell to her knees to gather a piece of Earth. Instead, she found a stone, for God had placed it there centuries ago, for her to find. Now it would become her means of hating Him. She picked up the stone as a man would grasp it, then found her feet. Her left eye was already trained into the heavens, right wrist cocked toward the throne room.

All agonies now shifted to the act of throwing. Every sinew, muscle, joint, and fragment of despair made ready the rock for the face of God. She would hit Him, yes. And her tongue, too, lay poised with the forbidden question, "What have You *made* me?!"

The stone traveled a little way into space, propelled by the impetus of the word "made." But then it returned to Earth, though she never heard where.

She had missed.

The forbidden question, however, had not missed at all. In fact, it had hit squarely, and she knew it. Something had happened. Now she felt millions of invisible eyes. She had unmistakably commanded something, perhaps everything. The field was now a stage. With knowledge of this came a liberating rush of boldness. If she was naked before the universe, then she would *be* naked. What happened next happened too quickly to stop.

Grasping her robes, she tore them aside to expose her breasts. These hung ample and perfect, bequeathed by the Placer of the Stone. Next, she withdrew a vial of olive oil from a small leather pouch around her waist, then turned it upside-down into her left palm. Shaking her breasts lightly back and forth, she cupped and slapped the oil to them. Everyone attended, yet not a star moved from its place above the distant row of acacia trees.

Now she gave it to God and to whoever else was up there. "This is what I am!" she cried. "This is what You made me!"

She let her arms fall to her sides, then shook her breasts back and forth before the Master Craftsman and His cohorts, faster and faster, harder, then harder still. Her breathing quickened to panting, her hair flew about her face, her waist hurt from the twisting. Surely, she was mad.

"Look at me!" her voice quavered. "This is what I am! This is what I do! This is what You made me!"

Less than a minute, and it was over. God, it was enough. No. It was too much. She wrapped the sections of clothes around her. Then, still heaving from her effort, she fell to her hands and knees in the field, weeping. The soil was indifferent to her tears. She, too, was soil. She did not dare look toward heaven now.

She waited very still for the strike that would kill her. She wondered if it would hurt. At least it would be fast, she thought. She would at least meet it kneeling, her face to the ground.

When would it come? Why was it taking so long? Perhaps the ground would part and swallow her. She wished it would hurry.

But the sky did not open, and the ground did not part. Rather, a saying came into her mind. This saying came uninvited, and wholly unimagined. It came distinctly, fashioned of only two words: "I know." These words calmed her enough so that she dropped her hands to her sides and fixed her eyes toward a faint glow to the East, above Jerusalem. The sun was coming up. Oddly, her agony felt dispelled. She felt warm now, as if an arm had been laid on the back of her neck and shoulders, sending warmth through her whole body. She even looked at her left shoulder, as if she would see a hand there, so real did it feel. But no hand was there. But an arm did lift her to her feet and the words came again, "I know," only this time they were followed by her name.

Scene II

Later that day, near midday, Mariba came to see her.

"I saw the Teacher!" Mariba said.

Mary was drinking a cup of coffee then, her fifth. "Jesus? Where?"

"He entered the home of Simon, the Pharisee. Maybe a half hour ago." (Luke 7:36—"Now a certain one of the Pharisees asked Him, that He may be eating with him. And entering into the Pharisee's house, He reclined.")

"That's it. I'm going there," Mary said. And she got up to leave.

"What do you mean, you're 'going there?'" asked Mariba.

"I'm going there."

"You can't just walk in. Let me tell you about him

first."

"I already know," Mary said. "I've heard." She was already at the door.

"What will you do when you get there?"

"I don't know yet."

"Are you completely mad?"

"What does it matter? He lives near the Tower of Mariamne, right?"

"Simon? Yes. But you'll never find his place."

"I'll find it." And with that, she was gone.

Scene III

(Luke 7:37-38—"And lo! A woman who was in the city was a sinner. And, recognizing that He is lying down at table in the Pharisee's house, fetching an alabaster vase of attar and standing behind, beside the feet of Jesus, lamenting, she begins to rain tears on His feet, and with the hair of her head she wiped them off and fondly kissed His feet, and rubbed them with the attar.")

Attar is an essential oil obtained from—flowers.

Jesus knew the timing. So when Simon finished a sentence that ended in "coming," the Teacher looked toward the door. Simon's glance followed His. Several seconds elapsed. What was He staring at? Then the door burst open.

Lo! A woman. She quickly scanned the room, looking for Him. Many eyes pierced her. But these, she did not care for. She looked only for the eyes of the Teacher. And she found them. No words were exchanged, or needed to be. Her eyes simply said, "I am here." His said, "I know."

A vase of attar sat next to the couch where Jesus and Simon reclined. She grasped it, no one rising to stop her. Then, coming around, she knelt at the feet of Jesus and began to rain tears upon His feet. She wiped the tears with her long hair. Then she kissed His feet, rubbing them with the attar.

Simon was aghast. He looked at the Teacher, Whose eyes were closed.

Simon looked pleadingly at one of his servants. Each knew what the other was thinking, thanking God for the privacy of thoughts, and for the Teacher's sealed vision.

(Luke 7:39- "Now, perceiving it, the Pharisee who invites Him said in himself, saying, 'This one, if he were a prophet, would have known who and what manner of woman it is who is touching him, seeing that she is a sinner.'")

Simon turned back toward Jesus with a false calm. Suddenly, Jesus' eyes locked onto him. "Simon, I have something to say to you."

The veneer of the Pharisee crumbled. "Teacher, say it!"

"Two debtors paying usury were owing a certain creditor. The one owed five hundred denarii, yet the other fifty. Now, they having nothing to pay, he deals graciously with both. Which of them, then, will be loving him more?"

"I take it that it is he with whom he deals the more graciously."

"Correctly do you decide." Jesus then gestured toward the woman with His left hand, His gaze still locked onto the man beside Him. "Are you observing this woman?"

"Yes, Teacher."

"I entered into your house; water for My feet you do not give, yet she rains tears on My feet and with her hair she wipes them off. A kiss to Me you do not give,

yet she, from the time I entered, did not intermit fondly kissing My feet. With oil My head you do not rub, yet she with attar rubs My feet."

"Teacher..!"

"On behalf of which, I am saying to you, pardoned are her many sins, for she loves much. Now to whom there is scant pardoning, there is scant loving."

Then, turning to the woman, Jesus said, "Go in peace."

Scene IV, some months later

The Teacher is now pinned to a Roman stake, dying. Rivulets of blood find the secret places of His manhood; he is naked. His mother is crying; someone named John is trying to console her. Several local women, too squeamish to approach, look on from the Gennath Gate.

But there are other people here laughing and taunting the crucified man. Surprisingly, these are the city's religious elite. They had become jealous of the victim because His love outworked their many rules and laws. His love changed lives that their laws and ceremonial washings never could touch. He ate with sinners, who worshipped Him. He raised some people from the dead, restoring sight to others. He said He was God's Son. The elite of Judaism knew this could not be.

In the middle of all this, with the sky darkening,

His mother crying, the priests laughing, John working in vain, and some Roman soldiers gambling for His last garment, the Teacher says:

"Forgive them, Father."

The earth can't stand it and quakes. A huge curtain in the temple, weighing hundreds of pounds, tears itself down the middle. A Roman soldier, awestruck at the sufferer's words and the other manifestations, breaks down at the foot of the cross. He throws down his helmet, kneels against the cross, pushes the top of his head against the wood to heave against it and cries:

"Surely, this was God's Son!"

Move the scene to a palm tree a few miles from Jerusalem. Move it to a cloudless day, near a lake. Put a picnic basket there, some happy kids, a few hot fish. "Forgive them, Father."

It doesn't work.

Try it at the temple, under a marble carving and a statue, with a few of the elders present and a man waving incense. Jesus is gesturing, His arm emerging from the soft folds of His tunic. "Forgive them, Father."

No effect.

Move it to the Pool of Bethesda; it's cool there and the bathers will make a ready audience. "Forgive them, Father."

Nothing.

Is there something wrong with the Script? Move the

scene back to the Place of the Skull.

"Forgive them, Father."

I am falling to my knees at the cross now, pushing the top of my head against the wood, to heave against it.

The Catholics kneel because of Him. The Pentecostals raise their hands. Baptist preachers get all sing-songy and glisten with sweat. All of this because the Creator of the world took flesh at Bethlehem. "Thank God He came!" is the cry of these earnest worshippers. The revelation of God's love has changed their lives. With Him, they have something to live for.

The worship session is over, however, and it's time for Phase 2. All must be damned now that has ever withstood Christ. The Catholics distribute flagellums and begin beating themselves (all right, most merely give up candy for Lent). The Pentecostals yell at Satan until he retreats behind a snare drum. The Baptists burn Pilate in effigy, along with some R-rated videos.

Only one thing is missing from this picture: Mature reflection. There would be no Christ to kneel before had not Sin invaded the world. And where would be the Crucified One without Romans practiced in that terrible art? And what becomes of His resurrection without an Adversary to ensure His death?

I would like, at this time, to make two statements. Some will consider these heretical, for they are logical; logic, we know, is the enemy of all religion. Nevertheless: 1) Since there can be no salvation without something to be saved from, sin is necessary, and 2) Since "all is of God"—2 Corinthians 5:18—and sin exists, then sin must be of God.

Wait.

Sin means "to miss the mark." Does God ever miss the mark? No, never. Therefore, God never sins. He cannot. I am not saying that God sins. But if God meant for sin to enter the universe, then He did not miss the mark when it came. He would only be a sinner if He didn't mean for sin to come, but it came anyway.

Some religious people, attempting to read this, will unfairly accuse me of making God a sinner. But have I called Him that? Not once. I have only said that sin must be of God. I reached this conclusion by logic, based on the scripture that says "all is of God."

I am a champion of the responsibility of God for whatever has entered His universe. Others would prefer to say: "God is not responsible." What a frightening doctrine—the irresponsibility of God.

But we like it.

So how did sin come about then?

By stealth and trickery, apart from God's original intention.

I don't suppose you see what you have just done.

Do we ever?

You have made God a sinner.

We would never do that.

You do it indirectly by making Satan sovereign in sin. God never intended for sin to mar His universe, according to you. Your unavoidable conclusion is that Satan disrupted God's original intention, forcing God into Plan B. God missed His original mark and settled for less. That's sin.

We're only trying to help God, to erase all the bad things from His résumé.

I know, but you're a public relations nightmare. By attempting to excuse God for doing what you cannot see a purpose for, you have booted Him from His throne.

How can you say that?

Everyone who tries to shield God from the consequences of His own creation inadvertently—yet inevitably—makes Him a sinner.

Are you trying to get logical on us?

I don't expect you to follow me. I'm doing this for the sake of my readers, who can still think. I want them to see that anyone who attempts to relieve God of responsibility for sin, ends up making Him the very thing they try to avoid.

And you have a better doctrine?

I'll say. My doctrine is that God is still on Plan A. This is the only doctrine that recognizes His deity. There is no contingency plan with the true God; there can't be. God meant for sin to come, therefore, He did not sin when it came. Sin had to enter this world, to play its part in fulfilling His purpose. What purpose? Revealing salvation. Salvation was part of His plan from the beginning.

Prove it.

Revelation 13:8 says that the Lamb was slain from the foundation of the world.

We hate that verse.

I know. You wish it wasn't there.

Darn you for bringing it up. It ruins our theology.

It opposes your theology. You say man's sin forced God back to His drawing board for a contingency plan: Christ. *Christ as a contingency plan?* How demeaning to the Son of God. Yet this is what your teaching of "Adam blew everything" leads to. Yet Revelation 13:8 proves that Christ's sacrifice predates Adam's sin. By this we know that God had sacrificial love in His heart from the beginning. Yet there can be no revelation of this apart from human failure. Christ was no afterthought. Jesus was not a good idea come late. Satan did not inspire Calvary by forcing God's hand.

Are you accusing us of making Calvary a result of God's

reaction to Satan?

Yes.

Okay.

Neither good nor God can be revealed without opposition. Since there was a time when no opposition existed in the universe, God had to create it. And He did. "I create evil," says the Lord God. That's Isaiah 45:7. What answer do you have for this verse?

We have no answer, and you know it. We spend all our free time trying to explain it away.

Yes, and the more you talk and try to explain God, the more people despise Him. That's because your explanations are all wrong. You can't believe this simple verse because you mistakenly assume evil and sin to be eternal. And so, because of you, many people actually believe that, long ago, God lost control of His universe, and He has been struggling ever since to salvage some of it.

We always did want to affect the world.

Then congratulations. Because of you, people wrongly believe that God is scrambling to keep up with the devil, running around the universe putting out fires, hoping to convince people to accept His wishful attempt at a rescue called Calvary. This is why most people think God is a lunatic and unworthy of serious consideration—because of you.

Ha, ha! God is running around the universe trying to put out fires!

You hurt our feelings.
You blaspheme God.
Is this why the world turns off our television shows and avoids our churches?
I'm guessing.
Oops! Gotta go! It's time for worship service!

God's program in a nutshell

What is the divinely appointed task of sin and evil? Simply stated, it is the work of contrast. God made creation to depend on contrast for revelation. Creation cannot know good apart from evil; it cannot know love apart from hate; it cannot know friendship apart from enmity. And as we saw with the prostitute at Simon's house, neither can it know grace apart from sin.

The plan is this: Give all creation a limited experience of evil, hate, enmity, and sin. This and this alone will prepare it for an eternal appreciation of good, love, friendship, and grace—all the things that are God. Temporary evil is bartered for eternal good. Fair enough?

Next, all creation is shown this good in the actions of a Man so full of love for them that He gives Himself to a degrading death He doesn't deserve, for their sakes. Bleed this Man with whips, nails, and spears. *Then* when He says, "Forgive them, Father," creation trembles and falls silent. Give Him that script at the temple, under a date palm, in a boat; it doesn't work. It works only as He is pinned naked to a stake before His mother.

With the love of God thus matted and framed, the Man dies with all our mistakes tied to His back. Then God raises Him from the dead victorious, all our missteps left behind, never to condemn us.

Thus vindicated and glorified, this Man eventually, through the eons, draws all creation to His feet, where they acclaim the greatness of God. The book of Philippians states that, in the name of *this* Man, "Every knee should be bowing, celestial and terrestrial and subterranean, and every tongue should be acclaiming that Jesus Christ is Lord, for the glory of God, the Father" (Philippians 2:10-11). The book of Colossians states that the blood of this Man, Jesus Christ, will reconcile and return a groaning creation, all creation, to God (Colossians 1:20).

With this goal accomplished, God trashes the whips, nails, and spears. All the sin and evil: gone. It is so. The last enemy God abolishes is death—that's 1 Corinthians 15:26. Since death is the last enemy abolished, all other enemies will have gone before, including sin. Please pardon the sheer logic of it.

I will never make light of sin. Speaking relatively, I realize the terribleness of opposing God. I realize the terribleness of sin. It is only when adopting the absolute viewpoint that I see a higher purpose in it, a purpose revealed to us in the scriptures. This is the viewpoint I choose to assume.

Those who say that sin will last forever are the ones making light of it. The doctrine of eternal torment is the doctrine of the eternal tolerance of God for sin. Apparently, God thinks so lightly of it that He will allow it to continue forever and ever. It is the teaching of eternal torment, not my teaching, that makes light of sin. I believe that when God is finished using sin, He will banish it from His universe. Scripture, correctly translated, confirms this.

The doctrine that leaves sin lingering eternally is the doctrine that treats it like a chocolate-covered marshmallow.

Failure by design

Frustrated with your failures? Feeling condemned? Can't overcome a bad habit? I've got great news for you:

"Now we have this treasure in earthen vessels, that the transcendence of the power may be of God and not of us" (2 Corinthians 4:7).

Your humble little vessel of sin is made that way on purpose. We are clay pots by design, not because we have gone afoul of God's intention for us. Let this revelation soothe the exhausted self-improver. Retire, Christian soldier! You fail by design, not because you are a failure. God wants you cognizant of the source of your power, and He has many creative ways of driving this home. One of these is sin.

Wouldn't some of us love to shed our earthenware now and still walk among mortals? Our sins keep us from producing a perfect walk, and we mourn this. What we do not understand is that an imperfect walk is the main idea of this life. God puts the treasure of His spirit in earthen vessels now to keep the vessels from situating themselves upon high places. A perfect walk is not what we need right now. Who could live with us? Could we stand ourselves? Humility is a blessed thing this side of resurrection. Vessels on high shelves sit poised, ready to topple and shatter upon hard floors. Pride is burdensome and is known for preceding falls. Can it be so bad to be delivered of this?

Thank God for the comfort of mistakes. Mistakes remind us of our clayhood and drive us toward Christ. When we finally quit chasing perfection and accept these vessels of clay, we will become happier. When we forget about ourselves, peace will ensue. The happy acceptance of imperfection is the beginning of easy breathing. Because, really, how can you be peaceful and flogging yourself simultaneously? You can't. That's why no one in a religion is truly happy. People in religions act happy because they're expected to, but they're only one step away from disappointing their deity and suffering his wrath.

How happy can they truly be?

I once heard a movie star on a talk show tap into this very thing. Ignoring the cameras, this star looked at the studio audience and said, "You people are lucky. You people don't know how good you have it. You look up here and envy me. Yet I am a miserable person. Everyone expects perfection from me, always. Revel in your anonymity, in your uncelebrated failings. You are blessed."

Somehow, I'll never forget that.

Little hands in the toyshop

Deliverance ministries think they're doing you a favor by trying to pray, pray, pray you out of your trials. These ministries thrive on you wanting a problem-free life. "I want the answer to my problem," is the pitch today that keeps these ministries at bat. I thank God for their track record of failure. What the poor seeker does not realize is that the problem *is* the answer, and that shedding the problem before its time would be disastrous.

Romans 8, verses 35 through 37, reads: "What shall be separating us from the love of God in Christ Jesus? Affliction, or distress, or persecution, or famine, or nakedness, or danger, or sword? According as it is written that 'On Thy account we are being put to death the whole day, We are reckoned as sheep for slaughter.' Nay! in all these we are more than conquering through Him Who loves us."

I have the word "in" highlighted in orange in my Bible so decisively that it leaks through three pages. You've got affliction? That doesn't belong to a Christian walk, so we'll get some people together and pray you out of it. You've got distress? There must be something wrong with your prayer life; ever tried a prayer circle?

And what's with this persecution business? You wouldn't be persecuted unless you were doing something wrong. As for nakedness, you're obviously lacking faith. If you had more faith, you could believe God for a pair of Levis and be the best-dressed person in your church. So what are you waiting for? Start conquering.

But is it *out* of all these things that we are conquering? No. Listen to Paul. Paul says that we are conquering *in* them. It is these very things that make us look to Christ. He conquered so that we wouldn't have to. We don't conquer by walking a trouble-free life or getting everything we want. We conquer by looking to Him who conquered sin and death on our behalf. 2 Corinthians 12:10 says, "Whenever I may be weak, then I am powerful."

Are you weak? Then you're powerful. Read the verse again. Are you weak? Then you're powerful. Why are you trying to become a Super Christian? Read the verse again. You're weak? Good, then you're powerful. You've arrived. *Hello?* You're a success.

The curse of President's Day

I used to work for the U.S. Postal Service. Most of the time, the mail was manageable. But the day after a Monday holiday, we'd open the door to find mailbags stacked to the top of our rifle racks. The mail moves

365 days a year. So while mail carriers are sitting at home nursing paper cuts, a double workload is waiting for them at the post office Tuesday morning. It's a potentially discouraging situation.

You've probably noticed this principle. When a job looks manageable, it's easy to jump in and manage it. "I can tackle this," you say, and in you go. Everybody loves a healthy challenge. But when a job looks impossible, it makes you want to go pour a cup of coffee, sit down, and stare at the job.

Rather than inspire us, the post-holiday workload deflated us. It was harder to jump into an impossible-looking task than one we thought we were up to. The first thing we always did, of course, was make a pot of Maxwell House.

This Postal Service analogy only goes so far. We couldn't stare at the mail for long. Eventually, we had to send it to the wrong zip code. But when God makes a job look impossible, He's not doing it to inspire us. He's doing it to relieve us of self-confidence, to make us draw a deep breath, and to cause us to focus our attention on Him. When a postal job looks daunting, the Postal Service applies more pressure. When a life-obstacle seems ready to crush us, the pressure is actually off us at that point (it's always off us, but we rarely realize this without a crisis) and God says, "How about *this* way?"

Human inability highlights divine strength

A guy once asked me: "How do you know that the Bible is the Word of God?"

"It's mainly a faith thing," I said. "We just believe that it is."

"I suppose it comes down to that," he said.

"But it's more than that," I told him. "If man had written the Bible, he would have put a better light on man. The Bible is a humiliating account of mankind. In scripture, man is always at the bottom, looking up. Do you think human beings would have written it that way? We'd have had us all in shiny blue pants, riding on the backs of elephants, cracking whips."

I couldn't have been more serious.

In the Bible, God is always getting humans into scrapes so that He can get them out of the scrapes and show His power. You say, "No, Martin. God isn't getting the humans into the scrapes. The humans are getting themselves into the scrapes." Well, that theory works fine until you consider accounts such as the hardening of Pharaoh's heart. And we're going to do that shortly. But first I want to show you how God delights in making things humanly impossible before He sets to work.

Remember the story of the blind man Christ healed? What is the first thing the Lord does? He spits on the ground, makes mud, and then smears the mud on the man's eyes. Then He tells the man to go wash in the Pool of Siloam. The guy comes back reading *The Jerusalem Post*. Just when you think God is crazy with this mud business, you start to wonder, *Maybe God is making a point. Maybe mud on top of blindness is God's way of compounding a problem.*

Consider First Kings, chapter 18, when Elijah challenged the prophets of the false god Baal to a contest, to see which God was real. Elijah and the prophets of Baal would each set up an altar. Each would pray to their God to send fire down to their respective altars. The God who sent fire down would be the true God. The prophets of Baal went first.

According to verses 26 of that chapter, the prophets of Baal "called on the name of Baal from morning until noon, saying, 'O Baal, answer us.' But there was no voice and no one answered. And they leaped about the altar which they made."

No Baal. It was Elijah's turn.

Notice the curious thing Elijah does to his altar. I'm quoting from verses 33-35. Elijah said, 'Fill four pitchers with water and pour it on the burnt offering and on the wood.' And he said, 'Do it a second time,' and they did it a second time. And he said, 'Do it a third time,' and they did it a third time. And the water flowed around the altar, and he also filled the trench with water."

With the dousing of the altar, Elijah, through the spirit of God, was setting up a field of "impossibility" on which God would demonstrate His power.

Is God making some things impossible for you? Is God dousing your life with water? And when you seem about to recover, is He dousing you a second time? Then a third time? Is there running water in the trenches of your life? Are you getting ready to put on your swimsuit, sit down, and stare at your insurmountable trials? Good. The sooner you do that, the better off you'll be. God has purposely dampened your life with impossibilities, in order to bring you to the end of yourself. The result is that you will be in a relaxed position (flat on your back, for instance, or on your face) to hear and see His new plan for your life.

1 Kings 18, verses 38 and 39: "Then the fire of the Lord fell, and consumed the burnt offering and the wood and the stones and the dust, and licked up the water that was in the trench.

"And when all the people saw it, they fell on their faces; and they said, 'The Lord, He is God; the Lord, He is God.'"

What a wonderful place to be. What a wonderful thing to say.

Cheaper by the dozen

Speaking of impossible situations, consider Israel. These are God's chosen people? At first, second, and third glance, it appears that God chose the wrong people. With Israel, it's one embarrassing scene after another.

Consider Joseph's brothers. They sell their own brother (Joseph) into slavery because they're jealous of their father's favor of him. Then they dip Joseph's coat in blood and tell Jacob (Israel, their father) that a wild beast killed him. What an incredible sin. And these are the forefathers of the celebrated tribes of Israel?

But years later, after Joseph has become great in Egypt and is used by God to save millions from a deadly famine, Joseph says to his brothers (Genesis 50:20): "But as for you, ye thought evil against me; but God meant it unto good." There you have it. God meant for those sons to do what they did. He meant for them to sin. You've never heard this message in church, I bet. But the apostle Paul verifies the truth in Romans 11:8 using the whole nation of Israel as an example, saying, "God gives them (Israel) a spirit of stupor." Note the active verb "gives." God doesn't merely allow Israel to have a spirit of stupor, as some say. Neither does God stand by and watch Satan stupefy the nation. No. Rather, God Himself gives Israel a spirit of stupor. Why in the world would God do this? Romans 11:11,12 provides the answer: "In their offense is salvation to the nations...their offense is the world's riches." Because of the sin of the eleven sons, a whole people was saved from a killing famine. Because of the offense of the nation Israel, salvation has come to you and me. So now you see why God is sometimes called the divine alchemist; He turns man's misses into His makes. In fact, man's misses *are* His makes. As soon as you realize that God eventually brings good from evil and sin, you can tolerate the process. May God grant you a spirit of farsightedness. Don't trip on God's processes. Look ahead toward the goals these processes are intended to bring about.

By Israel's weakness, God magnifies His power abroad. When God at last saves Israel herself, Israel will be able only to stand by, weep, and praise Him. There

May God grant you a spirit of farsightedness.

will be no back clapping among the sons of Jacob at the inauguration of the kingdom. Israel's sin is God's good. Seem too fantastic to be true? Romans 3:5 puts it in a tight package. Paul, speaking for the nation Israel, says: "Our injustice is commending God's righteousness." What a humbling thing, to be on the left side of that equation. But that's where we are, right along with Israel. God cannot save people who are not first sinners. And guess what our end of the contribution is? (Hint: It ain't the salvation end.)

Gideon and the banana milkshake

I like the story of Gideon in Judges, chapter seven. Gideon has an army of 32,000 men. This should be plenty enough to beat the Midianites. Unfortunately for Gideon, it's too many. The Lord tells Gideon in verse 2, "The people who are with you are too many for Me to give Midian into their hands."

Had I been Gideon, I might have asked, "Pardon me, Lord, but don't you mean that the people who are with the *Midianites* are too many?"

No, the Lord doesn't mean that at all. Let's let Him finish: "The people who are with you are too many for Me to give Midian into their hands, lest Israel become boastful, saying, 'My own power has delivered me.'"

Here's a plain illustration of the principle we've been discussing. God is planning on making it impossible for Gideon and Israel to win this battle. The result of this will be that the pressure will be off Gideon and Israel, and God will get the glory. Gideon doesn't come to this realization right away, however.

The first thing God does, in verse 3, is to have Gideon tell the people that whoever is afraid can go home. 22,000 honest people raise their hands. Now Gideon is left with only 10,000 men.

Okay, Gideon might have thought, *I think I can still whip the Midianites with ten thousand warriors.*

But God isn't finished. Verse 4: "Then the Lord said to Gideon, 'The people are still too many; bring them down to the water and I will test them for you there. Therefore it shall be that he of whom I say to you, "This one shall go with you," he shall go with you; but everyone of whom I say to you, "This one shall not go with you," he shall not go.'"

This is getting stranger by the minute, Gideon may have thought. *But, okay. I'll do what He says. How bad can it get?*

Bad.

Verse 5. "So he brought the people down to the water. And the Lord said to Gideon, 'You shall separate everyone who laps the water with his tongue, as a dog laps, as well as everyone who kneels to drink.'"

Verse 6: "Now the number of those who lapped, putting their hand to their mouth, was 300 men; but all the rest of the people kneeled to drink water."

Verse 7: "And the Lord said to Gideon, 'I will deliver you with the 300 men who lapped and will give the Midianites into your hands; so let all the other people go, each man to his home.'"

So there stood Gideon, his hands on his hips, watching 300 dog-lapping idiots wade from the river. *This is ridiculous,* Gideon may now have thought to himself. *I started with 32,000 warriors and now I've got 300 oddballs. But you know, this is so ridiculous that it'll probably work. Ha! I can't wait to see how God's going to pull this thing off. This'll be a piece of entertainment, if nothing else. All I know is, I'm done for. It's all up for me.*

When Gideon's army had been reduced from 32,000 to 10,000, Gideon was worried. But he was still gauging his strength, still confident, still in a fighting mode. When his army was reduced from 10,000 to 300, I can picture Gideon back at camp, drinking a banana milkshake in his hammock, staring at the stars. "Come to the war tomorrow," he says to a young assistant who had wandered near his tree. "It'll be a show you'll never forget. Don't know how yet, but it will be."

"But Gideon," the lad says, "you only got three hundred men."

"I know. A right lot too many, probably. I'd feel better with half a dozen. Oh, well. That's the way it goes, kid. Say. Fetch me another banana, will you?"

Here's how it happened the next morning: "And [Gideon] divided the 300 men into three companies, and he put trumpets and empty pitchers into the hands of all of them, with torches inside the pitchers. And he said to them, 'Look at me, and do likewise. And behold, when I come to the outskirts of the camp, do as I do.

"'When I and all who are with me blow the trumpet, then you also blow the trumpets all around the camp, and say, "For the Lord and for Gideon."'

"So Gideon and the hundred men who were with him came to the outskirts of the camp at the beginning of the middle watch, when they had just posted the watch; and they blew the trumpets and smashed their pitchers that were in their hands.

"When the three companies blew the trumpets and broke the pitchers, they held the torches in their left hands and the trumpets in their right hands for blowing, and cried, 'A sword for the Lord and for Gideon!' And each stood in his place around the camp; and all the army ran, crying out as they fled.

"And when they blew 300 trumpets, the Lord set the sword of one against the other even throughout the whole army; and the army fled as far as Beth-shittah toward Zererah, as far as the edge of Abel-meholah, by

Tabath."

If there's anything I can't stand, it's fleeing as far as Beth-shittah, toward Zererah. If there's anything more irritating than that, it's fleeing as far as the edge of Abel-meholah. Going by Tabath is more than I can usually bear. How embarrassing for the Midianites. How wonderfully humbling for Gideon. How glorifying for God.

Abraham considered his body. Bummer.

Let's talk about Abraham. God promises him a son. This tickles Abraham because it's all Abraham wants. Every Bible guy wanted a son.

So Abraham tries and tries, waits and waits. No son. Read all about it in Genesis, chapters 15-18 and 21, and in Romans, chapter 4.

Sarah feels bad about being unable to bear, not that it's her fault. But Sarah tells Abraham to "go into" her handmaid, Hagar. Abraham hates the idea, of course, but a man has to do what a man has to do.

Abraham "hates the idea," as seen in this photo.

Nine months later, Ishmael is born. I imagine Abraham passing out cigars. Sarah doesn't smoke, however, and is not too happy about the way things have worked out. But she acts happy, for the sake of Abraham and the guests. Abraham says, "Here's the promised seed!"

God says, "Well, no, Abraham. This one was produced by *your* strength. You're going to have another son, but the strength will be Mine."

Oh.

It's tempting to get frustrated with God here, asking why He would go through this lengthy trial when He could just as easily (easier, actually) have produced the promised seed the first time. But remember: God is always making matters humanly impossible first, so He can set up what He is going to do later. It's the same reason you're a sinner now. Why not just make you perfect and skip this humiliating sin part? It's simple, really. It's because you won't be able to enjoy perfection later unless you've been a sinner now. Everyone wants to be happy in heaven. That's normal. But then everyone wants to curse sin down here. What these folks don't realize is that their happiness there depends on their misery here. The joy of perfection rests on the misery of missing the earthly mark. So really, God isn't doing this sin thing *to* you, He's doing it *for* you. This imperfect life of yours is a backhanded favor.

"Just think how happy we're going to be in heaven."

A disturbed reader objects vociferously. It is Monty:

"Then why does God exhort us to do the right thing?"

Answer: You need to know what the right thing is, Monty. There must be a standard. How will you know you've fallen short if there is no standard? How will you know how righteous God really is? How will you know when you've arrived at perfection? You are assuming, I think, that God gives exhortations as a means of testing you, to see what you will do. You may be thinking that God puts forth these exhortations as a challenge, so that you can impress Him with your accomplishments.

Not so, Monty. This isn't about you; it's about God. Think of scriptural exhortation as a matting inside of which God intends to paint a masterpiece. These exhortations are God giving Himself an opportunity to show the world what He can do through you. What a difference between that and you getting an opportunity to show to the world what you can do for God. If you've still got religious bones in your body, what I just said will deflate you. And from the looks of it, you're losing a pound of air per minute. But when the spirit touches this thing, you'll become thrilled. Because how good will it feel to finally realize that you're not supposed to live like Jesus, but rather, that Jesus is supposed to live His life through you? What a difference. This marvel will progress in accord with God's timing, not yours.

Need scriptural evidence? Good. Philippians 2:13 says, "It is God Who is operating in you to will as well as to work for the sake of His delight." See? This is for God's delight, not yours. Not only that, but He's the one operating in you to do what He wants. Hard to swallow? Then Isaiah 26:12 will positively shock you: "Lord, Thou wilt establish peace for us, since Thou hast also performed for us all our works." So what's in it for you? Incredibly, you will get the reward for the good work. God is that gracious. You get the reward for doing something He operated through you.

God will make you perfect, Monty, it's just not time for it. Take heart. God will do a few wonderful things in you now to keep you from getting totally discouraged, but I guarantee you that He won't do everything. There will be some thing in your life that you never will get over until resurrection. There will be some bad habit—I guarantee you—that will plague you to the grave. Is it because you're a bad person or have no willpower? No. Stop condemning yourself. It's because God doesn't want you rid of the thing yet. Stop considering your problem a plague and you'll be on the path toward peace. Your problem isn't a plague; it's a necessary element of an earthen vessel. You're fighting God, Monty; no wonder you're so tired.

Remember 2 Corinthians 4:7? "Now we have this treasure in earthen vessels, that the transcendence of the power may be of God and not of us." Earthen vessels are sinning vessels. God is still on Plan A, Monty, and so are you. Here's

"You're not actually thinking of not condemning yourself, are you?"

a verse you will never hear in church: Isaiah writes in Isaiah 63:17, "Why, O Lord, dost Thou cause us to stray from Thy ways, and harden our heart from fearing Thee?" Want the answer? It's because we're *supposed* to walk imperfectly now. Don't you think God could make us sinless if He wanted to? He's God, for God's sake. He can do anything He wants. That we're not perfect should convince us that God doesn't want us that way (yet) and has purpose for our imperfection. Sit down and think, Monty: The only way you can rejoice in an eternity of perfection is by being imperfect down here.

There is a shout now from someone else in the audience: *Hey! Here is finally something I can attain to!*

I'm with you there.

Everybody: Don't you think Abraham and Sarah felt tremendous pressure to produce the promised seed? They obviously did, which is why Sarah told Abraham to have sex with her handmaid. Abraham and Sarah were in a "let's try anything" mode. But as I said—and as scripture attests everywhere—it delights God to wait until the human has exhausted his resources before He shows them Who's really in charge.

Isaiah 64:4 assures us that God works for those who wait. I believe the reverse is also true, that God waits for those who work. When the human finally says, "Well, that's it, I can't take it anymore. I quit," *then* God moves. Then, all the human has to do is marvel and enjoy the new program. Psalm 46:10 states it very simply and in contemporary terms: "Relax and know that I am God."

Hey. I can do this.

So Abraham waits some more. Sarah is now so old that she has canceled her subscription to *Woman's Day*. Even while feeling sorry for Abraham, I like what Scripture says about him next: "He considers his body, already deadened." That's Romans 4:19. After all, Abraham is a hundred years old.

I picture poor Abraham in front of a mirror, considering his body. He looks it up. He looks it down. He tilts his head to the left. He tilts it to the right. It entertains me to picture Abraham doing this. But I don't think Abraham needed a mirror to "consider his body" in the manner Scripture describes. Whenever Abraham lusted after Sarah during this time, he was thinking of her wheat biscuits.

Abraham slowly turns from the mirror. Then he

dresses and goes for a long walk. After a quarter mile, he feels a little better. After a half mile, he feels a whole lot better. The pressure is falling from his shoulders. He's done for. Abraham, finally, is in an "I give up" mode. This is exactly where God wants him. He's got no more tricks up his sleeve, this Abraham. But a sleeve without tricks is the happiest kind of sleeve I know. It blows easier in a breeze and isn't so hard to swing when you walk.

The next thing that happens stuns everyone, especially Abraham and Sarah. After having long given up on the magic of romance, Abraham has an urge one day. It's a tickly little thing that starts at his toes and works its way up. Now, you may have your own ideas about what Romans 4:20 means when it says that Abraham was "invigorated." All I'm telling you is that the Greek word here is *endunamoo*, and its compound elements are "MAKE-IN-ABLE." Let's just say that Viagra has nothing on God. Let's just say that, suddenly, Abraham has something in mind besides Sarah's culinary skills.

Abraham and Sarah have a child. A miracle baby? It's an understatement. They name the child "Isaac," which means, "laughter." Everyone laughs when Isaac is born. But it's not the laughter of "Hey, this is funny," it's the laughter of, "Can you believe this actually happened?" It's the laughter of shaking your head, removing your turban, and rubbing your eyebrows. It's the laughter that sends you to your bed crying and thanking God. It's the laughter of never having to trust mirrors again, of never being troubled any more by the "facts."

There was no cigar-passing this time around, if I failed to mention it. There were no cigars because this was not a human work. It was not a time for self-congratulations; such a time had long passed. God had waited until the humans were finished before He picked up the job. By doing it this way, God left nothing for the humans to do but enjoy the new process, applaud, and praise Him.

Hey. *I* can do that.

Who hardened Pharaoh's heart?

I tell people all the time that God hardened Pharaoh's heart. I guess I'm a glutton for punishment. But it doesn't take a genius to know that God hardened Pharaoh's heart, and this is perhaps why I've grasped the fact so readily. Exodus 4:21 has God saying, "I will harden Pharaoh's heart." To make sure we can't miss it, God then repeats this phrase throughout the account. Then Paul brings it home in Romans 9:17-18, to make sure nobody forgets it:

"For the scripture is saying to Pharaoh that 'For this

selfsame thing I rouse you up, so that I should be displaying in you My power, and so that My name should be published in the entire earth.' Consequently, then, to whom He will, He is merciful, yet whom He will, He is hardening."

And *still* people don't believe it.

I had the following conversation one day with a Christian acquaintance:

"Who do you think hardened Pharaoh's heart," I asked the acquaintance.

"Pharaoh hardened his own heart," the acquaintance said.

"But before Moses even went into Egypt, God said in Exodus 4:21 that *He* would harden Pharaoh's heart."

"Pharaoh's heart was already sufficiently hardened," the acquaintance said.

"But God says in Exodus 4:21 that *He* would harden Pharaoh's heart," I said.

"Pharaoh had a free will and hardened his *own* heart," the acquaintance said.

"But God says in Exodus 4:21 that *He* would harden Pharaoh's heart," I said.

"You must be in a cult," said the acquaintance.

Other people of this ilk will sometimes say, "But Martin, God wouldn't purposely harden someone's heart against their will, and we don't care *what* the scriptures say."

Is that ever a telling statement. Whenever I meet someone in the leg hold of such disbelief, I go ahead and give them more scripture in order to trouble them further. I give them Psalm 105:25, which says: "God turned their heart to hate His people." This refers to God turning the hearts of the Egyptians to hate the Israelites. After this, my soon-to-be ex-acquaintances usually say: "Martin, are you telling us that God causes people to hate other people?" to which I usually answer: "No. Psalm 105:25 is telling you that."

Before I return to Egypt, I want to bring up Isaiah 63:17 again. I already mentioned it before, but perhaps you thought it was a misprint. Either this *is* a misprint, or there are some important scriptural truths we're not confronting. I'm leaning toward the latter. In 63:17 of his prophecy, Isaiah says, "Why, O Lord, dost

Some of my acquaintences leave so quickly they forget their shoes and coats.

Thou cause us to stray from Thy ways, and harden our heart from fearing Thee?" Orthodoxy has no answer for this. *God causes people to stray?* You might want to stone this Isaiah fellow for blasphemy (or at least kick him off the church board) until you discover a second witness from Paul, who writes in Romans, 11:8: "God gives them (Israel) a spirit of stupor."

What these two gentlemen are doing is supporting what I've been telling you, that God uses sin to back-drop salvation. It may help you for me to remove the stumbling block (the common assumption) that God is sinning by causing these people to sin. He's not. The beauty of the thing is how God can cause people to sin without sinning Himself. He doesn't sin by causing people to sin because the sinning is an integral part of His plan.

Slather on some suntan lotion now and return with me to Egypt. I want to pay this Pharaoh fellow a visit.

Pharaoh not plague-oriented

The reason God hardened Pharaoh's heart is plainly stated in Roman's 9:17. I quoted it once, but I'll do it again: "For the scripture is saying to Pharaoh that 'For this selfsame thing I rouse you up, *so that I should be displaying in you My power, and so that My name should be published in the entire earth.*'"

God wants His power and name published throughout the earth, and The Ten Plagues and the mighty Exodus will accomplish this purpose. God wants Israel to sing about a miraculous delivery from Egypt for thousands of years, and an accommodating Pharaoh doesn't fit this scheme. Unfortunately, this Pharaoh is particularly spineless. For instance, Pharaoh hates insects. It especially annoys him that none of his magicians have invented the No-Pest Strip. When the plague of insects comes, Pharaoh is ready to give in. What about frogs? If there is anything Pharaoh dislikes more than flies, it's frogs.

Pharaoh: Where's my shaving mug?

Pharetta: The newspaper boy saw it hopping down Giza Street.

Pharaoh: Did I ever tell you how much I hate frogs?

What about the rivers turning to blood? If there is anything that makes Pharaoh madder than flies and frogs, it's this.

Construction manager/fishing buddy: Catch anything today, Pharaoh?

Pharaoh: Yeah. Three red corpuscles, two capillaries and a clot. Don't you have a pyramid to build?

After the first plague, Pharaoh is ready to wave goodbye to the Israelites. Ditto every plague that follows. Read the account for yourself in Exodus, chapters 7 through 12. It's almost comical. After each plague, Pharaoh cracks and decides to let the Israelites go. This supports what I've been telling you, that Pharaoh was weak. But then, just when the Israelites have cinched the straps of their backpacks, God hardens Pharaoh's heart and Pharaoh changes his mind. Of course, Pharaoh is completely unaware of the outside coercion.

Pharetta: I wish you'd let the Israelites go. These golf-ball sized boils aren't doing much for my looks.

Pharaoh: I know. I could drive that one on your nose three hundred yards in a headwind. I've had enough of these plagues. God only knows what's next. I'm letting these troublemakers go.

Pharetta: Now you're talking sense.

Pharaoh: They're out of here. I think maybe I'll just...wait a minute. There's a strange sensation overtaking my heart.

Pharetta: I told you to lay off the cream cheese.

Pharaoh: No, it's not that. I'm just getting all flushed inside. I'm getting angry that Moses thinks he can just wander in here and tell me what to do. Who does he think he is? And who is this God of his? I'm getting more upset about this by the second.

Pharetta: Pharaoh, please. You said you were going to—

Pharaoh: Ha! If these desert rats think they can tell *Pharaoh* what to do...

Pharetta: Here we go again. (An aside to the reader:)

"He used to be so accommodating."

As I've just demonstrated, people will go to obscene lengths to try to show that Pharaoh got stubborn of his own free will and hardened his own heart. But the honest reader, untrammeled by orthodoxy and able to think for him or herself, will confront the facts: God caused Pharaoh to withstand His revealed will, so that he would accomplish His hidden intention.

I think I recognize the problem here. If you think that Pharaoh ends up in the orthodox version of hell for eternity, then you'll have a hard time accepting God's responsibility for it. But God would be responsible for it, if Pharaoh died in his God-imposed hardness.

But if Pharaoh (1) is only a temporary vessel of dishonor, made by God as a foil to reveal His power—Romans 9:17-21; (2) is cut down at the end of this work—Romans 9:22; (3) is brought before the Great White Throne after the Millennium—Revelation 20:5, 11-12; (4) is judged there for his acts—Revelation 20:12; (5) is cast into the lake of fire, which is the second death— Revelation 20:14; (6) is delivered from the second death when death is abolished—1 Corinthians 15:26; (7) becomes, after all this time, a part of the "all in all" God is destined to become—1 Corinthians 15:28: and (8) a part of the "all mankind" that God is the Savior of—1 Timothy 4:10; then (1) the cross of Jesus Christ turns out to be quite potent after all—Colossians 1:20;

(2) God turns out to be a genius for using Pharaoh to
magnify His mercy—Romans 11:32; (3) Pharaoh ends
up with no complaints because he'll be with God for
eternity—Philippians 2:10; and (4) since God can do
this with Pharaoh, you can sit contentedly through the
funerals of modern unbelievers—Philippians 4:6-7.

PHARAOH ENDS UP WITH NO COMPLAINTS.
GOD IS RIGHTEOUS.

Contrast, yet again...

Don't leave this book until you're founded on the contrast principle. When God deals with man, He always uses contrast. Understand this, and the entrance of sin and evil into God's universe becomes fathomable. Understand this, and you'll always look ahead. Patience will replace panic at the dawn of understanding, and you'll see what God is up to.

Consider God's use of contrast, and the divine order of it:

- Sin comes first, then grace (Romans 5:20-21).
- Lostness comes first, then salvation (Luke 19:10).
- Death comes first, then life (1 Corinthians 15:36).
- Darkness comes first, then light (1 Peter 2:9).
- Disobedience comes first, then obedience (Romans 5:19).
- The soulish comes first, then the spiritual (1 Corinthians 15:44).
- Corruption comes first, then incorruption (1 Corinthians 15:42).
- Dishonor comes first, then glory (1 Corinthians 15:43).
- Infirmity comes first, then power (1 Corinthians 15:43).

Note that the shame of the former frames the glory of the latter. Never forget it. And this: Without the former, there *is* no latter. We've all experienced it.

Reader: Grace boggles my mind.

Martin: Only because of all the bad things you've done.

Reader: I love Spring sunshine. Spring sunshine makes my heart dance.

Martin: You can thank the long winter for that, and God's use of clouds.

Reader: Can you imagine the thrill for Mary and Martha, when their brother Lazarus emerged from his tomb?

Martin: It certainly makes a case for decomposition.

Reader: My mother died last year and I miss her still.

Martin: This temporary pain is preparing you for endless joy, when you see her again.

Reader: I bet your freedom in Christ just thrills you.

Martin: Yes, and there are so many priests I would like to thank, who made that possible.

Reader: Adam sure made a mess of things in the Garden of Eden

Martin: He set the stage for what Christ did at Calvary.

Reader: I'm so tired some mornings I can hardly get out of bed.

Martin: Think how good you will feel in your new body, when there's no more gravity.

Reader: Are you telling me that even *gravity* is priming me for endless bliss?

Martin: Yes. It's another temporary hassle.

Reader: Is there an IRS in heaven?

Martin: No.

Reader: Say no more!

How much sense does it make, then, to curse the corruption? To despise the darkness, death, toil, trouble, and shame? To despair of sin? To condemn what buys our future joy and happiness?

You can't know grace and good without sin and evil. You *can't*.

So now you know.

Strike three

It will help you to remember what we discussed earlier, that God will one day discard the dark side of these contrasts. The sickness, the death, the sin and the evil will do their duty, then depart. This is the opposite of what religion has told you. According to religion, the Christian religion included, there will always be a cauldron of evil, sin, and death to mar God's universe. If not for those of their camp, then for someone.

Wee-ha.

This nightmarish concept is the result of faulty translations of Scripture embraced by hardened hearts. But this is why otherwise normal people reject God's responsibility for sin and evil. This is why Christianity lays an apparently battered universe at the feet of the devil; they think sin and evil are eternal. Thus deluded, they've brazenly tried to help God by removing bad things from His résumé. God doesn't need the help. By "cutting God a break," they've cut into His throne instead. Rather than seeing sin and evil as Act I of a masterpiece, they've drawn the curtain too soon, putting a universe in chaos beyond His reach.

No. To think of evil, sin and death as endless is to rob these of their purpose in revealing God. For what purpose? I don't mind repeating it: That God may be "all in all" (1 Corinthians 15:28).

This is the grand purpose toward which God is marching.

Postscript: Practical Application
(Excerpted from an actual letter.)

Dear Rosemary,

First of all, relax. Everything you are going through is human. Nothing you are doing is shocking to God. Never mind what it does to me.

But God is not hanging over you with a giant fly swatter. You may have been taught in church that God regularly scans the earth with a giant fly swatter just looking for people who rub their hairy legs together. No. God is in the grace business now. These days, people who rub their hairy legs together get blessed, not cursed. You have childlike faith! You know who you are and do not hide yourself from God. You do not pretend you are something other than an irritating little creature that can't decide where to land. Can I tell you a story?

Melody and I were eating dinner at Olive Garden a couple years ago when we were accosted by a man who asked, "Would you like more breadsticks?" It was our waiter, whose name, we discovered, was Fred. My mother taught me never to talk with my mouth full of breadsticks, so I didn't say anything. Melody usurped her place as a submissive wife, however, and answered,

"More breadsticks would be fine, thank you." I don't recall her saying, "Tell us about your educational and career goals," but Fred proceeded to unfurl the wonders of the local seminary, where he was studying to become a man of God.

Seminary students unfurling their wonders invariably make me want to interrupt them. But I honored my crazy mother again. And so it was my authority-usurping wife who filled the conversational gap, clearing her throat and saying, "We're believers, too."

I knew we were in trouble. Melody's clear-throated statement had the same effect on Fred as the removal of the Dutch boy's finger had on the dike. Fred barraged

This is an artist's conception of Melody, Fred and me at the Olive Garden. Except for Melody's cap, my shoes, and the painting of the boxer on the wall, the artist got most of the details wrong. I am disappointed, and will not use him again. My apologies.

Melody and me with information about his college, about God, and about how happy Jesus was to be part of the Holy Trinity. In fact, we were barraged with everything but Coke and coffee refills. But Fred was only warming up to *this* shocking and barraging statement: "I'm amazed at how good God is to me when I'm living right. When I'm living right, God sort of pats me on the head and does many wonderful things for me."

Melody, meanwhile, had become bored, cynical, and extremely thirsty. "You mean like getting you more Coke?" she asked.

"No," said Fred. "Nothing at all like that."

I had reached my breaking point, and Fred sensed it. While he paused to fondle a set of ivory prayer beads dangling from his apron pocket, I seized the day with, "Imt's eben more abmfmazing what Goddoes wiff *me.*"

Fred was clearly agitated. "*What?*" he demanded. "What did you say, patron?"

I became serious and swallowed my huge ball of wheat paste. "I *said*…it's even more amazing what God does with *me.*"

Fred was so interested in what revelation I might offer that he rushed off to get Melody another Coke. So I said to Melody, "See, on the days I really screw up and sin like crazy, *those* are the days God chooses to do something wonderful for me. In this way, God stuns me with His grace and humbles me. What do you think about *that*?"

Melody rolled her eyes. "I already know about it," she said. "Now do you think you can wipe that grease off your lips and get me more salad?"

You're too worried, Rosemary. It's one thing to be a sinner, it's another thing to be worried about being a sinner. The apostle Paul recommends in Philippians 4:6 that you not worry about anything. This would include your sins. If Paul didn't mean for it to include your sins, he would have said, "Don't worry about anything except your sins."

I think you should formalize your divorce. Since you can't live with Billy, at least do this for the sake of the kids and the state of Oklahoma. In God's eyes, you are already divorced. They are not this reasonable in Oklahoma City.

Did I say you were already divorced? Yes. Look at 1 Corinthians. 7:10-11:

Now to the married I am charging, not I, but the Lord: A wife is not to be separated from her husband. Yet if she should be separated also, let her remain unmarried or be conciliated to her husband.

A few technicalities here will comfort you. In the Concordant Version of the New Testament, the "not," in the phrase "a wife is *not* to be separated from her husband," appears this way—**no**t—with a lightface "t" at the end. This means that the "t" is not in the Greek. Those Greeks. If all the letters were dark face, as in "**not**," this would be an emphatic "not," which says, "not ever, no way, no how." But with the lightface "t," this is less than emphatic. In fact, it's conditional. It says, "this is not recommended, but it may happen." (This is the Greek talking, not me.) In this case, it's obvious that it may happen because the apostle follows with, "yet *if she should be separated also*, let her remain unmarried."

Got it? Paul equates being separated with being unmarried. Watch how this works:

| ...if she should be | ...let her remain |
| **separated** | **unmarried** |

separated = unmarried

As sexual intercourse makes two people one in the sight of God (that is, it makes them married—1 Corinthians 6:16), thus also do separate addresses make them unmarried. But again, this occurs in God's eyes, not in the eyes of those at the state house.

Paul's recommendation, and mine, is that you either remain unmarried or reconcile with Billy. If you cannot reconcile with Billy, and you can't be without a man because of what Paul calls "being on fire," (that's scriptural terminology for "horny," 1 Corinthians 7:9), then you should marry the man you're with.

In any case, be at peace. "God has called us in peace" (1 Corinthians 7:15). Obviously, your situation is not ideal, but who can live the ideal? Fred is the only one I know of, but even he eats too many Olive Garden desserts. Paul said it is ideal for a man not to be touching a cheesecake (—whoops. I mean, "a woman," 1 Corinthians 7:1). So not even those of us who are married are living the ideal; I touch Melody all the time. But the apostle is not stupid, and he understands that "things happen" (namely, that women wear tight jeans and short skirts.)

So for the rest of 1 Corinthians, chapter 7, Paul mercifully deals with real situations and real people.

Yes, God did give us wine and pot and beer. I don't care for any of these, but the litter along the highway speaks of those who do. I think marijuana is illegal in Oklahoma. For this reason, you shouldn't smoke it. What kind of example are you setting for your kids? When the police drag you out of the house in handcuffs, who will make lunch? God gives us arsenic, too, but nobody takes it if they can help it. Smoking pot may give you a buzz, but it's bad for your lungs. I understand that if you have to smoke, you have to smoke. God does not condemn you for smoking pot. After all, Jesus Christ took away the sin of the world on the cross—John 1:29.

But your clothes will smell bad.

Things happen.
(1 Cor. 7:2)

I was recently invited to a guy's house who smoked. I was inside of his chamber of death for three hours. When I got home, I had to throw all my clothes in the hamper. The next morning, Melody said, "What happened to the hamper?" Even after I took a shower, my little beard thing still smelled like a forest fire. Boy was I mad. Melody wouldn't even kiss me. I hate it when a man is not allowed to touch a woman.

Rosemary, I just don't want you to be the sickest, stinkiest person ever lauded with grace.

Yes, God did give us wine. For all the Christians there at work who are reading this over your shoulder, I give you Psalm 104:13-15:

You are the One irrigating the mountains...From the fruit of Your works the earth is satisfied: You are the One making grass sprout for the beasts. And herbage for the service of humanity, To bring forth bread from the earth, And wine that makes the heart of a mortal rejoice, To make the face lustrous with oil, And bread that braces the heart of mortal man.

I do not think either "grass" sprouting for the beasts or "herbage for the service of humanity" refers to marijuana. The only members of humanity serviced by marijuana are...I can't think of any right now. But apparently there are some.

Beer and wine are fine in moderation. I used to hate the word "moderation," but now I merely dislike it. Nevertheless, it is sound advice. Whatever wine or beer it takes to get you happy, drink it. Then refrain. In one place, Paul recommends that his friend Timothy drink wine for his stomach and other infirmities—1 Timothy 5:23. A little wine, doctors are finding, is actually good for you.

God doesn't condemn people for getting drunk (who isn't tempted to "buzz off" this world now and then?), but the Bible still speaks against it. One of Paul's standards for a supervisor in the ecclesia was that he "not be addicted to much wine." Addicted to a little wine was all right, apparently. Alcoholism is a disease and should be treated as one. Not even humans condemn people for having diseases, so why would God? Jesus drank wine. His first miracle was turning water to wine. His second was explaining it to the Baptists.

Jesus never sinned His whole life. I honor and praise Him for that. It was a miracle; we can't manage it. So here is the good news: *You are not supposed to try to live like Jesus Christ.*

When I heard this, the first thing I wanted to do was maim all the people who told me over the years that I was supposed to live like Jesus. (Freako hypocrites. Did *they* live like Jesus Christ? Did *they* overturn Bingo tables and speak in parables? Did *they* call the Pharisees vipers and change the weather? Did *they* fellowship with sinners and die on a cross?) But then a wave of grace broke over my craggy heart and I decided not to maim the people. Instead, I would share my wonderful news with them.

I should have maimed them.

What a relief to discover that, rather than me being supposed to live like Jesus Christ, *Jesus Christ is supposed to live His life through me.*

WWJD is a snake pit with hairy spiders thrown in for agitation. Here is a recipe for frustration, guilt, and self-condemnation: WWJD. This question (What Would Jesus Do?), and the contemplation of it, may be why you smoke pot and shack up with Harry. What would Jesus do? He would not smoke pot or shack up with Harry, so forget trying to be like Him. This is what *you* do, probably because you are rebelling against an impossible standard hung around your neck by a nun, a Sunday school teacher, or a pastor who still thinks the Bible is a recipe book for moral behavior. Freako hypocrites. *The Bible is an account of the weakness of man and the strength of God.*

WWRD? That's right. What would Rosemary do? Why not just be yourself, Rosemary? Be good old flawed Rosemary who looks up to the mighty accomplishment of a perfect Savior. Jesus did something that you could not possibly have done. His work is supposed to make you sit and marvel at His work. Those who jump up and say, "I can do that!" are freako hypocrites who have not even approached a basic understanding of Christ's accomplishment.

God has not forsaken you. You are now constituted a sinner, so what else are you supposed to do but sin? Whatever grace God gives you, thank Him for it. Whatever moral problem He has yet to deliver you from, quit worrying about it. Do the best you can. When you fail, say: "Look at me, God. Look how badly I need you." When you succeed, say: "Look at me, God. Look at the amazing thing You did through my sorry vessel."

You have a conscience or you wouldn't have written me. God's hand is on you. You are not digging yourself into a hole, Rosemary. Jesus already did that for you. Then He emerged by God's power and left the sting of your sins behind Him, in the hole. You are setting the stage for God's performance. This is God's show, not yours. Will you upstage Him? Your contribution to the gospel is sin. His is salvation.

But I want you to be happy. Sin does not make you happy. So stop sinning if you can—you will be happier.

But don't battle so hard that you lose your peace. Only God knows which of your sins must remain for now. If you can't stop, then be at peace with your present condition. Can you do that? This is known as walking by faith, not sight. It is another recommendation of Paul's. It is recommended to sinners everywhere. I'm talking about 2 Corinthians 5:7.

Keep the faith, dear sister. Whatever you do, don't give up on God. You must continue believing in Him, in spite of what the clergy say. Do not think that God has given up on you. He lives for you. You make Him exercise grace—Romans 5:20—and He likes that. He lives to exercise grace. You are in God's hands and must accept that by faith, in spite of what you see.

I remain yours because of the grace of God. Trust me on this one.

Martin